The GOD
WHO WALKS
BESIDE US

The GOD
WHO WALKS
BESIDE US

DAVID ROPER

DISCOVERY HOUSE
P U B L I S H E R S°

Feeding the Soul with the Word of God

Discovery House Publishers is affiliated with RBC Ministries,
Grand Rapids, Michigan.

Requests for permission to quote from this book should be directed to:
Permissions Department, Discovery House Publishers,
P.O. Box 3566, Grand Rapids, MI 49501,
or contact us by e-mail at permissionsdept@dhp.org

Unless otherwise indicated, Scripture quotations are from the
Holy Bible: New International Version®, NIV®, © 1973, 1978, 1984
by Biblica, Inc.™ Used by permission of Zondervan. All rights
reserved worldwide. www.zondervan.com

Book design: Sherri L. Hoffman

Library of Congress Cataloging-in-Publication Data

Roper, David, 1933-
  [Jacob, the fools God chooses]
The God who walks beside us / David Roper.
     p. cm.
Previously published: Jacob, the fools God chooses. Grand Rapids,
MI : Discovery House, c2002.
  ISBN 978-1-57293-746-8
  1. Jacob (Biblical patriarch) 2. Bible. O.T.Biography. I. Title.
BS580.J3R66 2013
222'.11092—dc23

                                        2012032112

Printed in the United States of America
Second printing of this edition 2013

Contents

Introduction

To those who can't see it yet, everything
comes in stories, creating readiness,
nudging them toward receptive insight.

—MARK 4:11, *THE MESSAGE*

CHILDREN LOVE STORIES. When our three boys were small and Carolyn or I would tuck them in bed at night, they would always ask us to tell them a story. I'm happy to say our grandchildren are carrying on the tradition. "Papa," they plead, "will you tell me a story?"

Even grown-up children love stories. They touch our hearts in ways that raw data does not. They teach and the lessons are memorable, a fact that's especially true of the stories God tells in His Book, what John Milton called "the lives of men and women preserved and stored up . . . treasured up on purpose to a life beyond life."

God's stories are about the ways in which He takes ordinary people like Jacob and turns them into extraordinary beings. There are no self-made men or women. We are all *God's* workmanship.

Reading Jacob's story, then, is a little like looking over God's shoulder and watching Him at work. We can learn much from His handiwork.

Everything that was written in the past was written to teach us. (ROMANS 15:4)

DAVID ROPER

Boise, Idaho

have loved you," says the Lord. "But you ask, 'How have you loved us?'"

"Was not Esau Jacob's brother?" the Lord says. "Yet I have loved Jacob."

MALACHI 1:2

"I Have Loved Jacob"

God, who needs nothing, loves into existence wholly superfluous creatures in order that he might love and perfect them.
—C. S. LEWIS, *THE FOUR LOVES*

JACOB WAS BORN gripping his twin brother's heel, holding him back, trying to get ahead. That's why his father Isaac, with puckish, albeit prophetic, humor, named him Jacob—"heeler" in Hebrew—a verb that also means "to deceive."* It's the root of the adjective Jeremiah uses when he concludes, "The heart is *deceitful* above all things and beyond [human] cure" (Jeremiah 17:9, italics added).

True to his name, Jacob hustled his way through life, wheeling, dealing, double-dealing in unending efforts to promote himself. Shrewd, canny, devious, manipulative, and duplicitous, he had his own way of getting things done.

---

* The root word meaning "heel" is common to a number of Semitic languages, yielding a verb that means "to trip up," hence, "to deceive."

Jacob cheated his brother Esau out of both his birthright and his father's deathbed blessing; conned his father-in-law Laban out of much of his wealth; and flimflammed his way through life, playing one shell game after another. He pushed, shoved, and ran roughshod over anyone who happened to get in his way, alienating neighbors, family, and friends. He was a hard man to like.

Jacob, despite his failures and flaws
yearned for God with all his heart.

Esau, on the other hand, was "a skillful hunter, a man of the open country" (Genesis 25:27). He was rough-hewn but generous to a fault, quick to forgive, affectionate and jovial, good-hearted. (I'm not sure I can document all these attributes from the text, but that's the impression I get from reading his story and from what I know of Idaho outdoorsmen.) Esau was the kind of man you like to hunt, fish, and hang with—gutsy, gung ho, go-for-broke, full of high jinks, good humor, and every inch a man.

Yet there was this difference: Esau was a "profane" man (Hebrews 12:16 NKJV). He had no time for

God and no use for His plan to bring salvation to the world. Jacob, despite his failures and flaws—and they were many—yearned for God with all his heart, and God knew it.

Here's the thing: God does not foist himself on those who do not want Him, but He diligently looks for those who do, no matter who they are or what they have done. He seeks men and women, boys and girls, not because they're good and true, but because they *want* to be, and He wants to make them so.

God is never surprised by what we have done or what we're doing, nor is He alarmed by our struggles and failures along the way. He will not give up or go away until His work is done and we become, like Jacob, princes (see Genesis 32:28 KJV). "The one who calls [us] is faithful and *he* will do it" (1 Thessalonians 5:24, italics added).

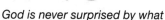

God is never surprised by what we have done.

Of the two brothers, Esau seemingly had the easier life. He lived in untrammeled ease and affluence throughout his entire existence, his good name intact to the end. Esau was a distinguished statesman who founded a long line of great kings (Genesis 36). For Esau, there was no "oak tree of weeping" (Genesis 35:8).

He [God] will not give up or go away
until His work is done.

Jacob never had it that good. Despite his aptitude for finagling, his entire life was a swarm of sorrow, pain, trouble, and care. Driven from his home as a young man, he lived for years in fear and weary loneliness. His first job—working for his equally devious father-in-law-to-be—was degrading and humiliating; his first marriage was a bitter disappointment, and the loss of his beloved second wife in childbirth a lifelong heartache. His children, whom he loved dearly, broke his heart. One by one he laid his loved ones in lonely graves as he mourned his lost hopes and dreams. We see him at the last, a weary old man, worn by anxiety and trouble, broken, disabled, displaced. "My years," he says in retrospect, "have been . . . difficult" (Genesis 47:9).

Yet Jacob was loved by God. And it was because of that love that he endured such searching discipline: "The Lord disciplines those he loves" (Hebrews 12:6).

Jacob was loved by God. And it was because of that love that he endured such searching discipline.

This discipline has always been the making of the man or woman God loves. No painful event can fatally injure us, nor can it long distress us, once we understand its purpose: God uses everything—suffering, sorrow, even sin—to draw us to Him and remake us in His image.

> Well mayest thou then work on indocile hearts;
> By small successes, disappointments small;
> By nature, weather, failure, or sore fall;
> By shame, anxiety, bitterness, and smarts;
> By loneliness, by weary loss of zest.
> The rags, the husks, the swine, the hunger
>   quest,
> Drive home the wanderer to the Father's breast.
> —GEORGE MACDONALD

As for Jacob, he experienced setbacks and tragic

failures of faith all along the way. If I were God I might well have considered Jacob a failed human being, a humbling embarrassment, and I most likely would have distanced myself light-years from him. Yet God was never ashamed to be called Jacob's God: Twenty-two times in the Bible He refers to himself as "the God of Jacob."

God, it seems, delights in this title that links His holiness with one so unholy. He does so because He does not want us to miss the message: He is the same yesterday, today, and forever. He feels toward us just as He did toward Jacob, and He is ready to do as much for us as He did for him, if only—if *only*—we will yield ourselves to Him, allowing Him to hold us and mold us in His hands.

God uses everything—suffering, sorrow,
even sin—to draw us to Him and
remake us in His image.

The Lord who was rich in mercy to Jacob is equally lavish to all those who call upon His name. No matter how flawed by deceit, how cursed by sin, how guilt-ridden, disgraced, and ruined we may be, we can be made new if we will only give ourselves to the mighty God of Jacob. "The LORD Almighty is with us; the God of Jacob is *our* fortress. *Selah!*" (Psalm 46:7, italics added).

> Thou know'st our bitterness, our joys are
>   Thine!
> No stranger Thou to all our wanderings wide!
> But yet Thou callest us Brethren! Sweet repose
> Is in that word—the Lord who dwells on high
> Knows all yet loves us better than He knows.
>
> —F. B. MEYER

This is the account of Abraham's son Isaac.

Abraham became the father of Isaac, and Isaac was forty years old when he married Rebekah daughter of Bethuel the Aramean from Paddan Aram and sister of Laban the Aramean.

Isaac prayed to the Lord on behalf of his wife, because she was barren. The Lord answered his prayer, and his wife Rebekah became pregnant. The babies jostled each other within her and she said, "Why is this happening to me?" So she went to inquire of the Lord.

The Lord said to her,

"Two nations are in your womb,
    and two peoples from within you will be separated;
one people will be stronger than the other,
    and the older will serve the younger."

GENESIS 25:19–23

The Choice

You are not an accident;
you are a divine choice.
—HENRI NOUWEN

JACOB AND ESAU had not yet been born when God fixed and foretold their futures: "The older will serve the younger." Here we have an early statement of that strange and difficult doctrine of election. Paul, in fact, makes God's choice of Jacob a paradigm of all those "splendidly illogical choices"* God delights in making (Romans 9:11–12).

Jacob was an essential link in God's plan to bring salvation to the earth.

To put it simply, and to avoid a pointless debate about God's inscrutable ways, may I say that *in this instance* Jacob's call was a call to serve, to be useful, to be part of the historic, spiritual line through

---

* A phrase from philosopher H. M. Hunter.

which the saving "seed" would be sown in a dark and dying world (cf. Genesis 3:15; 28:13–15; 35:10–12). Jacob was an essential link in God's plan to bring salvation to the earth.

God's call to serve is a call to suffer.

This reality, for me, explains the stern discipline through which Jacob had to pass, for God's call to serve is a call to suffer. Deep wounds seem the norm for those whom God is determined to use. Pain is needful, not for our sake alone, but also for those we are destined to serve. As Paul put it, "We who are alive are always being given over to death for Jesus' sake, so that his life may be revealed in our mortal body. So then, *death is at work in us, but life is at work in you*" (2 Corinthians 4:11–12, italics added).

These are the channels by which our souls are enlarged and our sympathies deepened.

"Death" is the inevitable, earthly lot of those whom God has called, the lonely, invisible burden of those whom God is using. Sickness, loneliness, clamor, unrequited love, incessant demands, and mundane duties—all conditions that seem to epitomize the frustrations of life—become the means by which the spirit of sacrifice and service begins to emerge in us. These are the channels by which our souls are enlarged and our sympathies deepened, the ways by which we are gradually conformed to the image of Him whose primary focus is (and always has been) on others. So death came to Jacob, and so it comes to us.

Our image of God's love is often simplistic. We picture Him soothing us, shielding us from harm, bearing us up to heaven on, as the hymn writer Isaac Watts would have it, "flowery beds of ease." We harbor no thought of the stern and robust reality of a love that employs the file, the forge, the hammer, the anvil; a seasoned love that can sustain the discipline by which everything false is driven out of us and we are made true.

Our image of God's love is often simplistic.

Such is the love of God that "teaches [disciplines] us to say 'No' to ungodliness and worldly passions, and to live self-controlled, upright and godly lives in this present age" (Titus 2:12).

When God wants to drill a man
   and thrill a man and skill a man,
When God wants to mold a man
   to play the noblest part;
When he yearns with all his heart
   to create so bold a man
   that all the world will be amazed,
Watch his methods, watch his ways:

How God relentlessly perfects
   whom he royally elects;
How he hammers us and hurts us
   and with mighty blows converts us
   into trial shapes of clay
   which only God can understand,
While our tortured heart is crying
   and we lift beseeching hands.

How God bends, but never breaks
   when his good he undertakes;
How he uses whom he chooses
   and with every purpose fuses us;
By every act induces us
   to try his splendor out—
God knows what he's about!

                —DALE MARTIN STONE

But why, we ask, would God labor so long and
arduously on a person like Jacob, who so often played

the fool? Well, I reply, is there any other kind of human being? We're all God's fools. Fools, in fact, are "God's theme," to borrow a phrase from Lord Byron. In His vast wisdom He has chosen to minister to the human race not through gilded saint or spiritual pros, but through a motley collection of past idolaters, adulterers, thieves, drunks, cheats, fornicators, perverts, prigs, and other sorry excuses for humanity (1 Corinthians 6:9–11).* It's not that He has to make do with the likes of us; it's that He has deliberately and with profound wisdom chosen us so that He might gloriously change us and display us before the whole world as holy exemplars of His handiwork.

He has deliberately and with profound wisdom chosen us so that He might gloriously change us.

Frederick Buechner marvels at the folly of God to choose for His holy work in the world a bunch of "lamebrains, misfits, and assorted odd ducks." Ah, the fools God chooses!

---

* According to Dorothy Sayers, God endured three great humiliations to save the human race: the Crib, the Cross, and the Church.

The boys grew up, and Esau became a skillful hunter, a man of the open country, while Jacob was a quiet man, staying among the tents. Isaac, who had a taste for wild game, loved Esau, but Rebekah loved Jacob.

Once when Jacob was cooking some stew, Esau came in from the open country, famished. He said to Jacob, "Quick, let me have some of that red stew! I'm famished!" (That is why he was also called Edom.)

Jacob replied, "First sell me your birthright."

"Look, I am about to die," Esau said. "What good is the birthright to me?"

But Jacob said, "Swear to me first." So he swore an oath to him, selling his birthright to Jacob.

Then Jacob gave Esau some bread and some lentil stew. He ate and drank, and then got up and left.

So Esau despised his birthright.

GENESIS 25:27–34

The Birthright

How poor was Jacob's motion and how strange
His offer! How unequal was th' exchange!
A mess of pottage for inheritance?
Why could not hungry Esau strive t'enhance
His price for a little? So much underfoot?
Well might he give him bread and drink to boot;
For toys we often sell our Heaven, our crown.
                              —FRANCIS QUARLES

ESAU TRUDGED BACK from a futile, frustrating day of hunting, so famished he was "about to die." He wasn't dying, of course; like all of us, he was prone to exaggeration at times.

Jacob was cooking up a mess of lentils, and the aroma filled the tent. "Give me some of that red stuff there!" Esau grunted as he stowed his gear. (Thus, the text says, he earned his nickname, "Red.")

Jacob, true to his perverse nature, replied, "First sell me your birthright."

"I'm about to die," reasoned Esau. "What good is the birthright to me?" So he swore an oath to Jacob and bartered his birthright away.

What was the birthright? It was Esau's spiritual inheritance, his claim to participation in the covenant God had made with his grandfather Abraham that through him and his descendants all nations of the earth would be blessed (Genesis 12:1–7; 13:14–17). It was the right of primogeniture, the entitlement of the firstborn son to be a link in the line of descent by which Messiah would come into the world. Through this lineage, Abraham's line had the privilege of holding and handing on to others the gift of salvation.

Esau had no hunger for God, no desire for
Love, no longing to give God's love away.

Jacob knew that Esau cared little for that birthright. Esau had no hunger for God, no desire for Love, no longing to give God's love away. He was a thoughtless and thoroughly secular man. Thus Jacob dared to make this extraordinary proposal—to exchange the God of heaven for a single meal. "How unequal was th' exchange!"

When Esau set more value on one meal than his
birthright, he lost his opportunity to be a blessing.

The author of Hebrews warns us not to be "immoral or godless like Esau, who for a single meal sold his inheritance rights as the oldest son" (Hebrews 12:16). The word translated "godless" ("profane" in some translations) means "to show contempt," carrying the connotation of one who tramples high and holy things. In his commentary on Hebrews, John Calvin suggests that the narrative of Esau's disdain "may be viewed as an exposition of the word 'profane'; for when Esau set more value on one meal than his birthright, he lost his opportunity to be a blessing." Esau sold out for so little; he trod "so much underfoot."

Waste no affection on those things that
should not be loved at all.

Long ago Augustine made the observation that "created spirits are capable of turning upward to God with their wills (conversion), or downward toward their bodies (aversion). Thus there are two distinct commitments of will—or two loves." There are those who know that life is bounded by realities beyond their grasp, who turn upward to God, who love first things first and secondary things second, and who waste no affection on those things that should not be loved at all. And then there are those who turn downward to gratify their primal and sensual drives—who grab and glut—who find themselves lost in their love for their "toys and lesser joys," as my wife, Carolyn, says. They are poor creatures absorbed in their poor loves, selling out for secondary causes.

What is my price? I ask myself. Could it be the tug of the elusive "good life"—wealth, power, prestige, position, security, style, the approval and praise of others? Could my sellout be a seduction, a casual fling, an "afternoon delight," a bartering of God's riches for a "single meal"?*

> And then comes a mist and a weeping rain,
> And life is never the same again.
>
> —GEORGE MACDONALD

Is that true? Will life never be the same again? The author of Hebrews concludes that Esau could "bring about no change of mind, though he sought the blessing with tears" (Hebrews 12:17). That sce-

---

* The Greek word for sexual immorality, *pornumi*, originally meant "to sell." The writer of Hebrews links *pornumi* with Esau's sellout: "See that no one is sexually immoral, or is godless like Esau, who for a single meal sold his inheritance" (12:16).

nario sounds ominous, as though one hasty act can turn God against us forever.

⌒∽

Though Esau must live with the
consequences of his decision, there
remained a way back to God.

The "change of mind" mentioned here, however, refers not to God's unwillingness to forgive but to Isaac's inability to reverse his decision. He had given the birthright to Jacob; he could not undo the act. But, though Esau must live with the consequences of his decision, there remained a way back to God, *if Esau had been willing to seek it.*

We can all recall days on which we've sold out— bartered away our spiritual legacy and plunged ourselves into ruin.

> We barter life for pottage, sell true bliss
>   for wealth or power, for pleasure or renown.
> Thus Esau-like our Father's blessing miss,
>   then wash with fruitless tears our fabled
>   crown.

—JOHN KEBLE

*Though the past is irrevocable
it is not irreparable.*

Our history, like all history, is unrepeatable. We cannot turn back the clock, redo or undo the wrong, though we seek to do so with tears. But though the past is irrevocable it is not irreparable. There is a fresh day before us, filled with new chances, opportunities, and expectations. God will not recant or recast the past, but He can and will forgive and set us on a new path. He will restore "the years the locusts have eaten" (Joel 2:25). He will provide us with opportunities to show how truly we have repented of the indiscretions of the past and how much we long to serve Him in the decisions to come. He will never mention the deeds by which we've shamed others and ourselves; once repented of, they are forgiven and forgotten forever. He will give us a place to begin again—to love, to serve, to touch others profoundly and eternally for His sake. This is the measure of our Father's forgiving love.

*God will not recant or recast the past, but He
can and will forgive and set us on a new path.*

28

"The end of all God's love for us," George Mac-Donald assures us, "is that we should claim our birthright."

When Isaac was old and his eyes were so weak that he could no longer see, he called for Esau his older son and said to him, "My son."

"Here I am," he answered.

Isaac said, "I am now an old man and don't know the day of my death. Now then, get your weapons—your quiver and bow—and go out to the open country to hunt some wild game for me. Prepare me the kind of tasty food I like and bring it to me to eat, so that I may give you my blessing before I die."

Now Rebekah was listening as Isaac spoke to his son Esau. When Esau left for the open country to hunt game and bring it back, Rebekah said to her son Jacob, "Look, I overheard your father say to your brother Esau, 'Bring me some game and prepare me some tasty food to eat, so that I may give you my blessing in the presence of the Lord before I die.' Now, my son, listen carefully and do what I tell you . . . so that [your father] may give you his blessing before he dies."

GENESIS 27:1–10

(Read Genesis 27:1–45)

The Upside of Sin

I's wicked I is; mighty wicked!
—HARRIET BEECHER STOWE'S
"UNCLE TOM"

ISAAC WAS GROWING "old and timey," as our grand-kids used to say, and thought he ought to settle his affairs, not the least of which was this matter of the inheritance. In bold defiance against God's will he determined that Esau, not Jacob, should receive the blessing. (The "blessing," I should note, was the final ratification of the inheritance.) And so Isaac called to Esau and urged him to hunt for game and bring it to him so he could eat it and bless Esau before he died.

Rebekah, overhearing Isaac's plan and wanting the best for her favored son, Jacob, had formulated a plot. Unknowingly, she was setting the stage for the undoing of Jacob. She urged him to outwit his father and secure the blessing for himself. Jacob, ever the opportunist, seized on his mother's unprincipled plan, deceived his befuddled old father, and got the blessing for himself. The rest, as they say, is history.

*Rebekah's plan was both a temptation
and a test for Jacob.*

Rebekah's plan, it seems to me, was both a temptation and a test for Jacob—a temptation to ratify his inheritance through dishonor and deceit, and a test of his willingness to wait for God to bless him in His own time and in His own way. The choice was Jacob's to make. And Jacob chose to forge ahead on his own, adding sin to sin and exposing his duplicitous and desperately wicked heart.

Jacob might have gone for years in dreamy self-content, thinking of himself as merely shrewd and savvy, his conscience untouched, ignorant of the appalling extent of his sin and continuing to take advantage of every opportunity without regard for principles or consequences. He perceived his shameful duplicity as mere peccadillo or, in Martin Luther's words, "puppy sin." He had to be brought to his senses.

*Jacob did not have to yield, but
yield he did, and in yielding stood
face-to-face with himself.*

So God permitted strong temptation to come Jacob's way. Jacob did not have to yield, but yield he did, and in yielding stood face-to-face with himself. For the first time, he glimpsed the sorry stuff of which he was made.

Temptation is sent to unveil the evils that lie deep within us.

This is a necessary step in soul-making. Temptation is sent to unveil the evils that lie deep within us, to reveal them to us and confront us with the truth of Nathan's terrible words to David: "*You* are the *man*!" (2 Samuel 12:7, italics added). Yet this revelation is just the beginning of all the good God intends to do for us, for before we can be greatly used by God, we must see the monstrous evil in our own souls.

This revelation is just the beginning of all the good God intends to do for us.

Jesus put it this way: "From within, out of men's hearts, come evil thoughts, sexual immorality, theft, murder, adultery, greed, malice, deceit, lewdness, envy, slander, arrogance and folly" (Mark 7:21–22). All the wickedness in the world lurks in us, undiscovered or disregarded, out of sight and out of mind.

God allows temptation and sin to show us who we are.

God allows temptation and sin to show us who we are; they are the means by which He makes us aware of all the unholy tendencies, motives, and appetites that reside within us. To know and to despair of ourselves is to know our need for God, the necessary prerequisite for handing ourselves over to Him for His healing.

To know and to despair of ourselves is to know our need for God.

Moral failure, thus, can be the first step toward godliness, for God uses every means, even sin, to bring about that good. On our own we could never detect or confront the evil in us. We must ask Him and allow Him to seek it out and destroy it. We should not be surprised, then, if in answer to our prayers for greater grace our Father should choose to hold up His undistorted mirror before our diseased and polluted souls. Instead of despairing, we should be glad.

John Newton understood:

I asked the Lord that I may grow
   In faith and love and every grace.
Might more of His salvation know,
   And seek more earnestly His face.

'Twas He who taught me thus to pray,
   And He I trust has answered prayer,
But it has been in such a way
   As almost drove me to despair.

I thought that in some favored hour,
   At once He'd answer my request,
And by His love's transforming power,
   Subdue my sins and give me rest.

Instead of that He made me feel
   The hidden evils of my heart,
And bade the angry powers of hell
   Assault my soul in every part.

"Lord, why this?" I trembling cried.
   "Wilt Thou pursue this worm to death?"

"This is the way," the Lord replied,
  "I answer prayer for grace and faith.

"These inward trials I employ
  From sin and self to set thee free,
And cross thy schemes of earthly joy
  That thou might find thy all in Me."

If of late you have begun to glimpse "the hidden evils of [your] heart," if you have discovered yourself capable of sins you never thought possible, if you have begun to loathe yourself, take heart. God is dealing with you, exposing the sham-person you are so He can begin to make you into the real person He has envisioned from eternity. He has begun a work that He will not abandon until you are presented faultless before His presence with exceeding joy (Jude 24).

God is dealing with you so He can begin
to make you into the real person He
has envisioned from eternity.

It was necessary for Peter's arrogant self-confidence to be uncovered in the high priest's courtyard so he could learn the true source of moral strength. It was necessary for Paul's pride to be exposed at Damascus so he could be made nothing—and thus become great. It was necessary for Jacob to see his own shameless, scheming heart so that he could utterly trust the One who would bless him and use him to bring salvation to others. If God is ever to make anything of us, we must know ourselves.

*Even though God permits failure in our lives,
He remains our advocate.*

Yet even though God permits failure in our lives, He remains our advocate. He will seek us out, as He did Jacob, shower us with His forgiveness, and assure us that He has work for us to do.

"Oh, *felix culpa* [happy fault]," Augustine exclaimed, that makes us better than ever before!

Jacob left Beersheba and set out for Haran. When he reached a certain place, he stopped for the night because the sun had set. Taking one of the stones there, he put it under his head and lay down to sleep. He had a dream in which he saw a stairway resting on the earth, with its top reaching to heaven, and the angels of God were ascending and descending on it. There above it stood the LORD, and he said: "I am the LORD, the God of your father Abraham and the God of Isaac. I will give you and your descendants the land on which you are lying. Your descendants will be like the dust of the earth, and you will spread out to the west and to the east, to the north and to the south. All peoples on earth will be blessed through you and your offspring. I am with you and will watch over you wherever you go, and I will bring you back to this land. I will not leave you until I have done what I have promised you."

When Jacob awoke from his sleep, he thought, "Surely the LORD is in this place, and I was not aware of it." He was afraid and said, "How awesome is this place! This is none other than the house of God; this is the gate of heaven."

GENESIS 28:10–17

Jacob's Ladder

That which is essential is invisible to the eye.
—ANTOINE DE SAINT EXUPÈRY

JACOB WAS ON THE RUN, fleeing from Esau's fury, lonely, desperate, and stripped of everything that gives meaning to human life, so lost that even God couldn't find him—or so he thought.

He came to "no particular place," as the Hebrew text suggests, and, because night was falling, cleared a spot on the rubble-strewn ground, found a flat rock on which to rest his head, and lay down. In misery and exhaustion Jacob soon lapsed into a deep sleep in which he began to dream. In this dream God thrust into Jacob's life a revelation of His great love, a timely and necessary disclosure for the dejected fugitive.

*In this dream God thrust into Jacob's life
a revelation of His great love.*

In his dream Jacob envisioned a stairway, rising from the stone at his head, connecting heaven and

39

earth. The traditional ladder is such a favorite image that it's a shame to give it up, yet it must be said that the picture of angels in their ungainly apparel scrambling up and down the rungs of a ladder leaves much to be desired. The term usually translated "ladder" actually suggests a stairway or stone ramp like those that led to the top of ziggurats, the terraced pyramids raised to worship the gods of that era.

The ziggurat with its steep stairway was essentially a symbol of man's efforts to plod his way up to God. One must trudge up a long, steep flight of stairs. It was hard work, but there was no other way to get help when you needed it (see Genesis 11:1–4).

The ziggurat with its steep stairway was
essentially a symbol of man's efforts to
plod his way up to God.

It's odd how that pagan notion of scrabbling and clawing our way *up* to God has found its way into our own theology and thinking. Some early Christian writers used the ladder as an analogy for spiritual progress, tracing the steps of Christian faith from one stage to another, rising higher by strong effort and good works—"grunting ourselves to God," as a friend of mine once put it. Walter Hilton's literary classic *The Ladder of Perfection* is based on that notion. The old camp-meeting song "We Are Climbing Jacob's Ladder" draws on the same association. In each case the emphasis is on the *ascent* of man.

What caught Jacob's attention, however, was not the stairway, but the fact that God was standing *beside* or *alongside* him, for that's the meaning of the preposition translated "above" in verse 13. (The same Hebrew word is translated "nearby" in Genesis 18:2 and "before," in the sense of "in front of," in Genesis 45:1.)

∽

What caught Jacob's attention was not the stairway, but the fact that God was standing beside or alongside him.

What is important to visualize is that God had come *down* the ramp. The God of Jacob's father, Isaac, and grandfather, Abraham, was at his side in this desolate place, contrary to Jacob's expectations and far from the traditional holy places he normally associated with God's presence.

"Surely the LORD is in *this place*, and I was not aware of it," Jacob declared with wide-eyed, childlike astonishment. "This [place] is none other than the house of God; this [stairway] is the gateway of heaven" (Genesis 28:16–17, italics added).

Jacob got the message in the metaphor, but God was taking no chances. He highlighted the picture with a promise that would sustain Jacob through the weary days of character-building ahead: "*I am with you* and will watch over you wherever you go . . . *I will not leave you* until I have done what I have promised you" (Genesis 28:15, italics added).

He highlighted the picture with a promise that would sustain Jacob through the weary days of character-building ahead.

This is our promise as well. "God has said, '*Never* will I leave you; *never* will I forsake you'" (Hebrews 13:5, italics added). He is present with us, whether we know it or not—in our joys but also in our sorrows; in our triumphs as well as in our confusion, disappointments, failures, frustrations, and bad judgments. While God is molding us, His love surrounds us—waiting, longing to make itself known.

God's presence is not a symbol, a manner of speaking, or a virtual reality, but the real thing—as real as it gets, as real as it was in the days of His incarnation. The difference is that now He is invisible to all but the eyes of faith.

◆

While God is molding us, His love surrounds us—waiting, longing to make itself known.

In the upper room Jesus promised His disciples, "I will not leave you as orphans; *I will come to you.* Before long, the world will not see me anymore, but you will see me" (John 14:18–19, italics added).

Some say that Jesus was speaking of His second coming, but I think He was and is concerned with this present age in which He walks with us unseen. He is actually (not figuratively) with us, spiritually visible to those who love Him. "He who loves me will be loved by my Father," Jesus said, "and I too will love him and show myself to him" (John 14:21).

"Would not this be a good day for the Lord to come?" asks one of George MacDonald's characters. "Aye," replies his fellow-traveler, "but is not this a good day for him to be walking beside us?" This rejoinder captures the essence of Jesus' promise.

Think, for example, of our Lord's post-resurrection appearance to the two disciples on the road to Emmaus. You know the story—how He fell in with them as they walked, expounding the Scriptures along the way. Then, when invited to eat with them, He "took bread, gave thanks, broke it, and began to give it to them" (Luke 24:30)—at which point, I suppose, they caught sight of the nail prints in His hands. "Then their eyes were opened and they recognized him, and he disappeared from their sight" (Luke 24:31). Or, as the text states literally, "He became invisible to them." He was *present* but unseen.

Or think of that day when He met again with His disciples in the upper room. He did not walk through the door or come in from the outside. He simply appeared, already with them in the room, *present* but unseen.

∽

This requires a determination to believe against all odds and all evidence that our Lord is actually beside us every moment of every day.

And so we, like Moses, endure, "because [we see] him who is invisible," the author of Hebrews insists (Hebrews 11:27). This is a perspective that requires a certain "obstinacy of belief," as C. S. Lewis would have it—a determination to believe against all odds and all evidence that our Lord is actually beside us

44

every moment of every day. There is no moment when we are alone.

Our Lord himself lived in continuous, conscious awareness of His Father's presence. "I am [never] alone," He said, "for my Father is with me" (John 16:32). That is the secret of His—and our—rich tranquility.

When we know our Lord is present, we experience a delightful sense of peace no matter what our circumstances may be. A serenity and security envelop us; foes, fears, afflictions, and doubts recede. We can forebear in any situation because we know "the Lord is near" (Philippians 4:5).

We, like Jacob, must practice God's presence, often pausing in the midst of our busy days to remind ourselves, "The Lord is here." We live surrounded by unseen realities, but our eyes are too often blind. Oh, that by humility and purity we might see Him who is invisible and see Him everywhere. "From youth we have only one vocation," says George MacDonald, "to grow eyes."

G. K. Chesterton was once asked by a reporter what he would say if Jesus were standing beside him. "He is," Chesterton replied with calm assurance.

Now Laban had two daughters; the name of the older was Leah, and the name of the younger was Rachel. Leah had weak eyes, but Rachel was lovely in form, and beautiful. Jacob was in love with Rachel and said, "I'll work for you seven years in return for your younger daughter Rachel." . . .

So Jacob served seven years to get Rachel, but they seemed like only a few days to him because of his love for her.

Then Jacob said to Laban, "Give me my wife. My time is completed, and I want to lie with her." . . .

When morning came, there was Leah! So Jacob said to Laban, "What is this you have done to me? I served you for Rachel, didn't I? Why have you deceived me?" . . .

Jacob lay with Rachel also, and he loved Rachel more than Leah. And he worked for Laban another seven years.

When the Lord saw that Leah was not loved, he opened her womb, but Rachel was barren. Leah became pregnant and gave birth to a son. She named him Reuben, for she said, "It is because the Lord has seen my misery. Surely my husband will love me now."

GENESIS 29:16–17. 20–21, 25, 30–32
(Read Genesis 29:1–30:24)

Home Schooling

The ills we see—
The mysteries of sorrow deep and long,
The dark enigmas of permitted wrong
Have all one key;
This strange, sad world is but our Father's
    school;
All chance and change His love shall grandly
    overrule.

—FRANCIS R. HAVERGAL

DESPITE THE ASSURANCE of countless fairy tales, there's no direct causal relationship between getting married and living happily ever after. Things go wrong—and sometimes terribly wrong. Despite the best of intentions, we may find ourselves in a house full of resentment, hostility, unrest, and misery. There is no heartache quite like that of an unhappy marriage.

Consider Jacob, who soon saw domestic tranquility deteriorate into bickering, bitterness, and hatred. His dysfunctional household tore his heart

47

to shreds. Yet Jacob's difficult marriage to Leah was just another phase of his spiritual formation, for God uses everything, even flawed and failed marriages, to get His hands on us and shape us into the men and women He has envisioned.

Some find family life to be their source of greatest satisfaction. Others find that its reversals, torments, and puzzles lead them to contemplate the meaning of life for the first time. But a challenging marital relationship can be our schoolhouse, the means by which we become conformed to His will, until we are finally living in, by, and for Him alone.

I know of no one who has entered into intimacy
with God who has not at one time or another
lost something thought to be indispensable.

Indeed, I know of no one who has entered into intimacy with God who has not at one time or another lost something thought to be indispensable. "What an ordinary person sees as necessary to have, God may take away from a person He is purifying," noted the seventeenth-century theologian Fenelon. And sometimes it is the love of one's life.

It is when other loves grow cold and still that we can begin to hear God's still, small voice whispering His love. It's when we lose the love we are sure we cannot do without that God gives us a love we cannot lose. As John Bunyan's Christian in *The Pilgrim's Progress* retorted to Obstinate, his detractor, "All that you forsake is not worthy to be compared with a little of what I am seeking to enjoy."

It is when other loves grow cold and still that we can begin to hear God's still, small voice whispering His love. It's when we lose the love we are sure we cannot do without that God gives us a love we cannot lose.

God often puts us into situations that seem to frustrate every hope of life, progress, and growth. Someone with much love to give finds herself in a marriage in which that love is unrequited. Another longs to bring peace to his home, yet lives in an atmosphere of unrelenting unrest, clamor, and confusion. The circumstances seem so meaningless and the efforts futile and impossibly difficult. Yet God knows exactly what He's doing. We must trust Him and submit to His will without struggling to escape. We only make life more painful for others and ourselves when we resist His hand. As Amy Carmichael put it, "In acceptance lieth peace."

We only make life more painful for others and ourselves when we resist His hand.

This is not to say that we must accept physical, sexual, or emotional abuse, or situations that endanger our children or ourselves. There are legitimate biblical bases for separation and divorce, although it's not my purpose to discuss them here. Suffice it to say that adversity does not in and of itself constitute a reason to break free. We must remain yielded, waiting for God's shaping, and knowing all the while that He loves us deeply. God's "unfailing love surrounds the [one] who trusts in him" (Psalm 32:10). No one could love us more. The comfort that comes from knowing we are held close in this kind of love is inexhaustible.

The comfort that comes from knowing we are held close in this kind of love is inexhaustible.

A difficult marriage can, however, provide a setting in which God can confront us with our skewed sense of self-importance. We begin to see ourselves for who we really are—not nearly as thoughtful, patient, polite, gracious, giving, and self-controlled as we have imagined ourselves to be. At best, marriage challenges these flattering illusions; at worst, it shatters them. We come to see how incurably ruined we are. Indifference, harshness, and coldness are the crosses on which our self-love begins to die.

We don't know to what extent Jacob's difficult marriage drew him toward God. Perhaps, at this stage of his life, not at all. But we do see in Leah's poignant story a snapshot of one who, in her suffering, found herself in God. Unattractive and foisted on a husband who neither loved her nor wanted her, Leah pined for a love that never came. Few stories are more moving than her secret history and the profound heartache revealed in the names she gave her sons (Genesis 29:31–35).

In her suffering, [Leah] found herself in God.

She gave birth to her first son and named him Reuben ("Seen"), for she reasoned, "The LORD has

51

seen my misery. Surely my husband will love me now." But he didn't.

Leah conceived again and gave birth to a son whom she named Simeon ("Heard"), "because the LORD heard that I am not loved." But Jacob still did not love her.

Again she conceived and gave birth to Levi ("Attached"), for "now at last my husband will become attached to me." But he didn't.

Leah conceived again and gave birth to Judah ("Praise"), vowing, "*This time* I will praise the LORD" (italics added).

Jacob never loved Leah, but her longing for love was as satisfied as it can be in this life, for she had God and His perfect love. Oh, I'm certain she had times of great loneliness and days when her heart yearned for human love. Yet God was always there to comfort her, for God in time "satisfies the thirsty and fills the hungry with good things" (Psalm 107:9).

We're made for love—to love and be loved. But what of those whose love is never requited by a spouse? Must they wither away in loneliness and despair? No, they can still know perfect love and satisfaction, for God's love endures forever.

This is not to say that God will banish all our pain

in this life. But our pain can lead us into a deeper love—the love of God—and greater fulfillment than we ever thought possible. And on ahead lies heaven, where our joy will be complete.

Our pain can lead us into a deeper love—
the love of God—and greater fulfillment than
we ever thought possible.

If you are among the ranks of the unloved in this life, don't run from your pain or try to manufacture or manipulate love. Instead, give yourself to knowing God and loving Him. Let your deep need for affection and caring draw you into His heart. "He gives a greater grace"—greater than anything you could ever gain on your own.

> Life is only bright when it proceedeth
> Towards a truer, deeper Life above;
> Human love is sweetest when it leadeth
> To a more Divine and perfect Love.
>
> —A. A. PROCTER

And here is multiplied grace: When we find ourselves enveloped in God's love, we are free to give ourselves in simple, pure love—even to the one who has caused our pain.

I'm haunted by a story about F. B. Meyer, that wonderful old saint whose writings always encourage and enlighten me. Meyer once confided to a friend that he felt welcome in any home in England but his own. His loveless marriage was a source of deep heartache for him, yet Meyer believed that he, through his aching soul, was being prepared by God to give love and strength to others—and especially to his wife at the end of her days. He wrote to her:

> If then your future life should need
>   A strength my love can only gain
> Through suffering—or my heart be freed
>   Only by sorrow from some stain,
> Then you shall give, and I will take
>   This crown of fire for Love's dear sake.

Ignore the voices that tell you to set yourself free. They are nothing more than the echoes of self-love and will only lead you to greater emptiness and misery. "Remain," as the apostle Paul urges in 1 Corinthians 7:20. "Stick the landing," as my bush-pilot friends love to say. God is working through your heartache, working against your intentions and desires, but pressing you in His direction, holding you with His affection, molding you to His perfect design. There is no greater love.

After Rachel gave birth to Joseph, Jacob said to Laban, "Send me on my way so I can go back to my own homeland. Give me my wives and children, for whom I have served you, and I will be on my way. You know how much work I've done for you."'

But Laban said to him, "If I have found favor in your eyes, please stay. I have learned by divination that the Lord has blessed me because of you." He added, "Name your wages, and I will pay them." . . .

Jacob heard that Laban's sons were saying, "Jacob has taken everything our father owned and has gained all this wealth from what belonged to our father." And Jacob noticed that Laban's attitude toward him was not what it had been.

Then the Lord said to Jacob, "Go back to the land of your fathers and to your relatives, and I will be with you" . . .

Then Rachel and Leah [said to Jacob], "Do we still have any share in the inheritance of our father's estate? Does he not regard us as foreigners? Not only has he sold us, but he has used up what was paid for us. Surely all the wealth that God took away from our father belongs to us and our children. So do whatever God has told you."

GENESIS 30:25–28; 31:1–3, 14–16

(Read Genesis 30:25–31:16)

Mild in the Wrong

Firm in the right; mild in the wrong,
Our heart, in every raging throng,
A chamber shut for prayer and song.
—George MacDonald

Fourteen years of faithful service to Laban had netted Jacob exactly nothing. Though his work had enriched his father-in-law, Jacob himself was as poor as the day he had arrived in Haran.

So, to provide for his growing family and their return to Bethel, Jacob agreed to shepherd Laban's flocks for six more years. At the same time, though, he made the modest request that he keep all the streaked, speckled, spotted, or off-colored animals for his wages.

The arrangement was clearly in Laban's favor. And Laban, anticipating P. T. Barnum's conceit that there's a sucker born every minute, readily assented to the deal. He insisted on making the selection himself, handing over Jacob's motley flock to the care of his own sons and driving them a three-day journey away to prevent crossbreeding.

But Jacob, ever the schemer, resorted to ancient magic to outwit his father-in-law. Laban countered by repeatedly changing the terms of their original agreement (Genesis 31:7, 41). In the midst of these machinations Jacob's flock became more numerous and stronger than Laban's, and he became very wealthy.

It wasn't Jacob's superstition that paid off.
It was God and His grace.

It must be said, however, that it wasn't Jacob's superstition that paid off. It was God and His grace. Sometime after Laban and Jacob had made their initial agreement, the angel of God had assured Jacob in a dream that *He* would be Jacob's protection (Genesis 31:12–13). In the end Jacob would say to Rachel and Leah, "The God of my father has been with me . . . [and] has not allowed him [their father, Laban] to harm me" (Genesis 31:5–7).

Here I pause to reflect . . .

There are those who exploit the trust of others, who prey on the unwary, who even use the name of God in support of self-serving schemes. But we never need to fear them. Even if they cheat us and change our wages ten times, God is with us, as He was with

Jacob, and will not allow them to harm us. Oh, they may take our goods, but they cannot touch our hearts because God keeps us eternally secure.

Certainly we can use the courts and other legitimate means to seek redress against injustice, and we can and must protect our families and ourselves from evil. But when we have done all we can do, the only thing left is to wait patiently for God to avenge the wrong. God, not those who defraud us, will have the last word.

∽

God will have the last word.

And He *will* render judgment on those who abuse His children (Genesis 31:42). This may not happen in this world, for He is full of compassion and does not desire that anyone should perish (2 Peter 3:9). But if those who exploit us do not call upon our Lord for forgiveness, they will not "stand in the judgment" (Psalm 1:5).

Dante finds thieves and swindlers in the lowest and most dismal levels of his *Inferno*. Although I don't altogether subscribe to Dante's vision of hell, I do share his conviction that unrepentant chiselers and cheats will fall into the hands of the righteous God.

ᙜ

When defrauded, we can take shelter
in God's righteous judgment and
wait for His vindication.

So, when defrauded, we can take shelter in God's righteous judgment and wait for His vindication. "The LORD is with [us] like a mighty warrior; so [our] persecutors will stumble and not prevail. They will fail and be thoroughly disgraced; their dishonor will never be forgotten" (Jeremiah 20:11).

Furthermore, in His time God will see to it that we're compensated by a grace infinitely greater than the degree of injustice we've suffered. The renowned commentator Matthew Henry notes: "Those that find men whom they deal with unjust and unkind shall not find God so, but, some way or other, He will recompense the injured, and be a good pay-master to those that commit their cause to Him." We may not gain the cause we sought, but we will attain the satisfaction we sought in the cause, and he who is well-satisfied is well-paid.

It's natural to desire to defend ourselves against injustice and to retaliate against the unjust, but, though it sounds odd these days, we can allow ourselves to be humbled. If we're long-suffering and forgiving when others misuse us, we'll grow in grace more quickly. God wants to work in us, as in Jacob, those things that are unnatural for us. Anyone can be patient when everything's going his or her way. The greater accomplishment is to be "mild in the wrong"— unruffled and forbearing under provocation.

∽

Anyone can be patient when everything's going his or her way.

Fenelon, the seventeenth-century theologian and chaplain to the court of Louis XIV of France, wrote: "Don't be so upset when evil men and women defraud you. Let them do as they please; just seek to do the will of God . . . Silent peace and sweet fellowship with God will repay you for every evil thing done against you. Fix your eyes on God. He's the One that afflicts or comforts you through people and circumstances. He does this for your benefit."

For *our* benefit? Indeed. Injustice helps us deal with our anxiety, intensity, instability, pessimism, and other negative manifestations of our sinful flesh. We learn to be tranquil and strong under duress. And if we feel we must litigate, we can do so with courtesy and dignity.

The apostle Peter writes for our encouragement: "It is commendable if a man bears up under the pain of unjust suffering because he is conscious of God. But how is it to your credit if you [do] wrong and endure [a punishment]? But if you suffer for doing good and you endure it, this is commendable before God. To this you were called, because Christ suffered for you, leaving you an example that you should follow in his steps . . . He did not retaliate; when he suffered, he made no threats. Instead, *he entrusted himself to him who judges justly*" (1 Peter 2:19–23, italics added).

We may despair of our cause, but we should never despair of God.

We may despair of our cause, but we should never despair of God. He will judge justly. We can instead submit to His will with a humble heart and let Him work out all things for us. The things that look impossible will be accomplished in His time with no help from us.

We only unsettle ourselves when we try to avenge ourselves. Why do we fret so under injustice? Why do we care what foolish and sinful men and women do to us? Is it not that we place too much value on money, position, success, and power? Don't we have a terrible fear that we will be deprived?

∽

Things that look impossible will be
accomplished in His time.

If so, we must pray again and again with Augustine in his *Confessions*: "Heal me of this lust of mine to always vindicate myself."

Careless seems the great Avenger; history's
    pages but record
One death-grapple in the darkness 'twixt old
    systems and the Word;
Truth forever on the scaffold, Wrong forever
    on the throne,—
Yet that scaffold sways the future, and, behind
    the dim unknown,
Standeth God within the shadows, keeping
    watch above his own.

                  —JAMES RUSSELL LOWELL

Then Jacob put his children and his wives on camels, and he drove all his livestock ahead of him, along with all the goods he had accumulated in Paddan Aram, to go to his father Isaac in the land of Canaan . . . So he fled with all he had, and crossing the River, he headed for the hill country of Gilead.

GENESIS 31:17–18, 21

(Read Genesis 31:17–55)

The Walkin' Man

The woods are lovely, dark and deep.
But I have promises to keep,
And miles to go before I sleep,
And miles to go before I sleep.
—ROBERT FROST

THEN THE LORD said to Jacob, "Go back to the land of your fathers and to your relatives, and I will be with you," (Genesis 31:3). God spoke and Jacob felt a sudden, passionate impulse to put Haran behind him and go home.

God knew that Jacob needed to go. His unrelenting efforts to increase his wealth were riddling his soul with ambition and greed. His wives, infected with the idolatry of the land, were in danger of corrupting him and their children. Jacob was beginning to forget who he was and the promises of which he was the heir. It was time for him to hit the road.

We too hear the highway calling. In the midst of our frenetic efforts to better ourselves here on earth, we sense a sudden hankering for something more—a curious discontent, a restless urge to move onward to a better place.

It's in the heart that we find the highways to Zion.

Our feet get to itching—or is it our hearts? For it's there in the heart that we find the highways to Zion. "Blessed are those . . . who have set their hearts on pilgrimage" (Psalm 84:5).

The journey begins with a vague longing, a gnawing, elusive hunger for our heart's true home. We may not be able at first to identify the tug, but it's nothing less than our Father's voice calling us away from this world: "Get up, go away! For this is not your resting place" (Micah 2:10). Like Ulysses, Frodo, ET, and Jacob, we too want to go home.

The journey begins with a vague longing
for our heart's true home.

In Jacob's case the wanderlust began with Laban's hostility. For some time their relationship had been strained, and now there were symptoms of a more serious disruption: "Jacob noticed that Laban's attitude toward him was not what it had been" (Genesis 31:2).

God will use anything to get our attention.

God will use anything to get our attention. It may be, as it was with Jacob, a change affecting a relationship—a much-loved child turning away from us, a long-term marriage unraveling, an old friendship fading away. It may be some prize we attain that leaves us feeling dissatisfied and empty, or something we lose that leaves us brokenhearted. It may be a change we cannot avert or a circumstance we cannot change. But whatever comes our way, we can be sure God's love is behind it, helping to pry our fingers loose from this decaying earth and drawing us toward Him and our eternal home.

When our hearts respond to God's call we
can be sure of opposition.

When our hearts respond to God's call, however, we can be sure of opposition. When Christian in *The*

Pilgrim's Progress determined to seek the City of God, his friends and family "thought that some frenzy distemper had got into his head" and tried to dissuade him. When he wouldn't be deterred, they "thought to drive away his distemper by harsh and surly carriage to him; sometimes they would deride, sometimes they would chide, and sometimes they would quite neglect him."

There was something of this in Jacob's journey. Apparently he thought Rachel and Leah would resist leaving, for Jacob fortified himself with strong arguments—a strange amalgam of cant and truth (Genesis 31:4–16). In his efforts to persuade them that they should leave Paddan Aram, we catch another glimpse of Jacob's cunning and crafty mind.

[God will] go before us, making the crooked straight, and the rough smooth. —F. B. Meyer

He could have saved his breath. God had been at work for some time to prepare their hearts, and Leah and Rachel at once assented to his plan. "If we would only go forward in simple obedience," F. B. Meyer writes, "we should find that there would be no need for diplomacy; [God will] go before us, making the crooked straight, and the rough smooth."

In Laban's march to stop Jacob, we see a vivid picture of the drive with which others will come after us to detain us (see Genesis 31:22 ff.). In Laban's objections we hear their disapproval. They wheedle and cajole. They threaten and jeer. They play on our compassion. They point out our hypocrisy and insincerity. They brush off our commitment as merely a fad or a phase we'll outgrow in time. But in the end they cannot hinder us. We have the reminder of God's assurance to Jacob: "I will be with you" (Genesis 31:3).

And then there's that anxiety that grips us at the outset of any uncertain adventure. *Am I up to the task?* we ask ourselves.

Of course we're not. Whoever thought we were? But once again God has promised, "I will be with you." Though we are confused at times, we're always underway. Though our feet may take us down paths we should not travel, we don't need to go back and start over. We can turn from our straying, follow our Guide back to the path of obedience, and go on from there.

Sometimes giving up seems easier than going on, but when things get difficult, we can rest for a while and renew our strength. There's an arbor on the Hill Difficulty, says John Bunyan in *The Pilgrim's Progress*, in which we can catch our breath before continuing the climb. And there's a scroll in the arbor which, when read, reminds us of God's love, His continual presence, and His sustaining power. There, His Spirit breathes within us a second wind.

Sometimes giving up seems easier than going on, but when things get difficult, we can rest for a while and renew our strength.

Then we must say to ourselves, "I will get up and go on." (All God's true children say the same thing.) There is no going back. Once we've set our hearts on pilgrimage, we can never again be content with this world or anything in it.

And so we walk on with our Lord—talking, asking, listening, trusting, waiting—moving each day a few more miles up the trail. God only knows where the trek will take us, but we have His calm assurance, "I am with you."

Once we've set our hearts on pilgrimage, we can never again be content with this world or anything in it.

This pledge is not hyperbole, metaphor, or some other figure of speech. God is the real thing—more real than any other companion—and His promise is just as sure. There is not one hour without His presence, not one mile without His companionship. That makes the journey lighter, easier on the legs and heart. As Izaak Walton's *Piscator* put it, "A good companion on the road makes the way to seem shorter."

When you need an extra measure for the load
    you cannot bear;
  When the road demands another mile or two;
There is grace sufficient, mounting on the
    wings of prayer,
  With extra measure God will meet you there.
               —AUTHOR UNKNOWN

J acob also went on his way, and . . . sent messengers
ahead of him to his brother Esau in the land of Seir,
the country of Edom. He instructed them: "This is what
you are to say to my master Esau: 'Your servant Jacob
says, I have been staying with Laban and have remained
there till now. I have cattle and donkeys, sheep and goats,
menservants and maidservants. Now I am sending this
message to my lord, that I may find favor in your eyes.'"

When the messengers returned to Jacob, they said,
"We went to your brother Esau, and now he is coming to
meet you, and four hundred men are with him."

GENESIS 32:1, 3–6
(Read Genesis 31:1–23)

Less Than the Least

This on my ring,
This by my picture, in my book I write:
Whether I sing,
Or say, or dictate, this is my delight.

Inventions rest,
Comparisons go play; wit use they will:
"Less than the least
Of all God's mercies" is my poesy still.
—GEORGE HERBERT

WE PRAY BEST when we have nothing going for us. "The best disposition for praying," said Augustine, "is that of being desolate, forsaken, stripped of everything."

Consider Jacob. When messengers announced Esau's advance, Jacob, filled with fear, began to pray:

O God of my father Abraham, God of my father

---

* A "poesy" is a short motto—in this case the motto that was engraved on George Herbert's ring and with which he signed his books: "I am unworthy of less than the least of all God's mercies."

Isaac, O LORD, who said to me, "Go back to your country and your relatives, and I will make you prosper," I am unworthy of all the kindness and faithfulness you have shown your servant. I had only my staff when I crossed this Jordan, but now I have become two groups. Save me, I pray, from the hand of my brother Esau, for I am afraid he will come and attack me, and also the mothers with their children. But you have said, "I will surely make you prosper and will make your descendants like the sand of the sea, which cannot be counted" (Genesis 32:9–12).

Jacob began and ended his plea by reminding God of His promise: "You said!" (Genesis 32:9, 12).

"Ah, he had God in his power then," F. B. Meyer reflects. "God puts himself within our reach in His promises . . . He cannot say nay—He must do as He has said."

God had promised to be with Jacob and bring him back to the land (Genesis 28:13–15). Thus Jacob could appeal to God's word. The Lord had promised to protect him, and He is the only One who *cannot* lie (Titus 1:2 NASB).

God is true. What He has promised He will do. We can rest in the integrity of His word. But we must be sure that we stand on God's *actual* word when we claim a promise, for then and only then do we have the assurance that God will come through. He is bound to do only what He has said He will do—nothing more or less.

Naïve, uninformed faith can be dangerous. I have a friend whose older brother once assured her that an umbrella had enough lift to hold her up if she would only "believe." So "by faith" she jumped off a barn roof, fell twenty feet straight down, and knocked herself out. And then, because she believed that the problem was a failure of faith, she tried again with precisely the same result. She got the message the second time around!

Faith must be informed—grounded on a clear understanding of what God has actually said.

Faith must be informed—grounded on a clear understanding of what God has actually said. Faith has no power in itself. It counts only when it is based on a plain and unambiguous promise from God. Anything else is wishful thinking.

Case in point: God has promised, "Ask whatever you wish, and it will be given you. This is to my Father's glory, *that you bear much fruit*" (John 15:7–8, italics added).

This is not an unequivocal promise that God will respond affirmatively to every prayer we utter, but rather a promise that He will grant every longing of ours for the fruit of the Spirit—love, joy, peace, patience, kindness, goodness, faithfulness, gentleness, and self-control. If we hunger and thirst for holiness and ask Him for it, He will begin to satisfy us. That's a promise we can count on, and "God don't make promises He don't keep," as Bob Dylan once pointed out.

Next, Jacob moved to confession: "I am unworthy of the least of your love"* he prayed, using a word for "least" that suggests the tiniest object. "Deliver me!" (Genesis 32:10–11 NASB).

What an odd juxtaposition: "I am unworthy of salvation. Save me!"

Unlike those who have it all together, Jacob realized that anything he brought to God had already been ruined by sin. He saw himself as the man least worthy of God's grace. Yet he could pray for mercy, for his hope lay not in his own worth, but in the promise of God to look with favor on those who throw themselves

---

* This is the first occurrence in history of this wonderful word for God's unfailing covenant love. Significant, is it not, that it comes from the lips of one who saw himself as so unworthy?

in penitence at His feet. Humility and contrition are the keys that open the heart of God.

Humility and contrition are the keys that open the heart of God.

Authentic prayer is a "crying out of the depths" (Psalm 130:1). It wells up from the soul that acknowledges its own deep depravity. Such prayers are offered by those who are thoroughly convicted of their sin and shame, but at the same time convinced of God's grace that flows forth to undeserving sinners. God hears best those who cry out like the tax collector in Jesus' parable, "Be merciful to me, *the* sinner!" (Luke 18:13 NASB, italics added).

Yet, isn't it odd? Jacob had scarcely finished his prayer of contrition and trust when he resorted to his earlier tactic, relying again on his own ingenious scheme for self-preservation (Genesis 32:7–8, 13–21). It would have been better for Jacob to wait for God to show him *His* plan. This would have led him in ways he could never have imagined.

Not so odd, however, as I think about it. Jacob is just like me.

So Jacob was left alone, and a man wrestled with him till daybreak. When the man saw that he could not overpower him, he touched the socket of Jacob's hip so that his hip was wrenched as he wrestled with the man.

Then the man said, "Let me go, for it is daybreak."

But Jacob replied, "I will not let you go unless you bless me."

The man asked him, "What is your name?"

"Jacob," he answered.

Then the man said, "You name will no longer be Jacob, but Israel, because you have struggled with God and with men and have overcome."

GENESIS 32:24–28

(Read Genesis 32:24–32)

The Breaking

A little east of Jordan,
Evangelists record,
A Gymnast and an Angel
Did wrestle long and hard.
—EMILY DICKINSON

IT WAS MIDNIGHT. "In great fear and distress," Jacob sent his family across the Wadi Jabbok so he could be alone. Then, in that dark, lonely place "a man wrestled with him till daybreak." And there, old Jacob finally met his match.

Jacob and the stranger brawled through the night, pounding and punishing one another, rolling in the dust, a fall to one and then the other. When dawn approached and the man saw that Jacob would not surrender, "he grasped the socket of Jacob's hip so that his hip was wrenched as he wrestled" (Genesis 32:25).

Completely expended, Jacob could no longer continue. But neither would he let go! Out on his feet, he still clenched his antagonist fiercely.

"Let me go," his opponent shouted, but Jacob

continued to cling. "I will not let you go unless you bless me," he said.

The man asked him, "What is your name?" The form of the question actually means, "What is the *meaning* of your name?"

"Jacob," he answered. Clever, cunning Jacob knew well who he was.

Then the man said, "Your name shall no longer be Jacob [the deceiver], but Israel [one who prevails with God] because you have struggled with God . . . and have *prevailed*" (Genesis 32:28–29, emphasis added). Jacob's defeat and victory came simultaneously.

Phantom match or real encounter? Jacob knew. His opponent was the Angel of the Lord, God himself,

coming to grips with Jacob's duplicity,

chastening his pride,

challenging his tenacity,

wrestling with him,

relentless in His love.

He would not give up until Jacob gave in and clung to God alone.

This clash was the climax of Jacob's lifelong ambivalence, resisting God and yet relying on Him. Now, utterly defeated and exhausted, Jacob gave up and gave in. Old Jacob was finished. He could no longer survive without a vice-like grip on God, clutching Him, clinging to Him.

Jacob was given a new name; the old name was passé. He was no longer Jacob but Israel—a winner. "The bewildered gymnast," says Emily Dickinson, "had worsted God." God had broken Jacob, and Jacob had won! "So Jacob called the place Peniel, saying, 'I have seen God face to face, and my life has been saved.' The sun rose above him as he passed Peniel [Hebrew, *Penuel*], and he was limping because of his hip" (Genesis 32:30–31).

⁓

His combativeness turned at last to dogged dependence upon God. Jacob was a new man.

Jacob went on his way dragging his leg, but the sun was rising on a new day and a new life for the man whom God had subdued. All craft and cunning were gone, his combativeness turned at last to dogged dependence upon God. Jacob was a new man.

Rabbi Neziv Berlin translates the name of the place where this encounter occurred, *Peni–el*, as "I have seen God." He then notes the change to the third person plural, *Penu–el*: "*They* have seen God" (Genesis 32:30–

81

31, emphasis added). Perhaps, he reflects, Jacob's spiritual descendants will see what he saw.

Indeed we do. His story is ours. We too want God—somewhat—but we hold out against Him. He knows He cannot prevail against us unless He takes some severe measure that will give us no alternative but to yield. And so He becomes our adversary—against us because He is for us. "Our greatest victories are wrought through pain and purchased at the cost of the humbling of the flesh," wrote F. B. Meyer. That's when we learn that "the secret of prevailing with God and man [is] not in the strength, but in the weakness of the flesh." So it was for Jacob; so it is for us.

Jacob's wrestling, though a literal match, was symbolic of the spiritual struggle that occupies us. It has to do with our hesitancy toward God; we place limits on how much of us He can have.

Jacob's wrestling was symbolic of the
spiritual struggle that occupies us.

Because God so loves us, He does not want to lose us. And so He pits His strength against ours. He will touch whatever it is that causes us to stand against Him. Our dreams may fail, our businesses may fold, our best-laid plans may go awry. An accident may impair us, a crippling disease might ruin us, or we simply grow old. Our bodies, once strong, begin to weaken; our minds, once sharp, begin to fail. He has touched us and stripped us of our natural strength and ability.

These effects are not signs of God's wrath and displeasure but evidences of His love. He is working through all of this, wrestling with us, dusting us up, bringing us down to take from us all that hinders His love. He will not give up until we're wholly His.

Jacob limped away from his encounter diminished, "halting on his thigh." His maiming marked him forever. But if you were to ask about his infirmity, he would tell you that the best day of his life was the day God put him on the mat. That was the night Jacob lost everything he had and gained everything worth having.

> Contented now upon my thigh
> I halt, till life's short journey end.
> All helplessness, all weakness, I
> On Thee alone for strength depend.
> —CHARLES WESLEY

⧢

After Jacob came from Paddan Aram, he arrived safely at the city of Shechem in Canaan and camped within sight of the city. For a hundred pieces of silver, he bought from the sons of Hamor, the father of Shechem, the plot of ground where he pitched his tent. There he set up an altar and called it El Elohe Israel . . .

Then Jacob said to Simeon and Levi, "You have brought trouble on me by making me a stench to the Canaanites and Perizzites, the people living in this land. We are few in number, and if they join forces against me and attack me, I and my household will be destroyed."

GENESIS 33:18–20; 34:30
(Read Genesis 33:18–34:31)

Two Steps Forward,
One Step Back

*Give us this day the daily manna, without
which, in this rough desert, he backward
goes who toils most to go on.*

—DANTE

JACOB, BOUND FOR Bethel, came to Shechem, a Canaan-
ite enclave. There he sank a well, settled in, and lost
his grip on God.

His family paid the price. They were swept into
idolatry, immorality, violence, and the gross mythol-
ogy that characterized that crude and cruel society
(see Genesis 35:2).

Read the record: Dinah, Jacob's only daughter,
"went out to visit the women of the land," as the text
puts it; or, as Jewish historian Josephus surmised,
sneaked out one night to party with her Canaan-
ite girlfriends. The incident led to her rape and to
the ruin of her brothers, who in retaliation deceived
and massacred the men of Shechem, then looted the

city. All of this made Jacob's name "a stench to the Canaanites and Perizzites, the people living in this land."

Jacob, called to be a blessing to the nations, plagued them instead with a curse—and this after his historic, life-changing encounter with the Angel of the Lord at Wadi Jabbok (the brook Jabbok).

Why did the reborn Israel revert to the rogue Jacob? Why do *we* regress? Some profound spiritual experience stirs us to the core of our being, and we think we are changed forever. But despite our determination, promises, and vows, we revert again and again to the old way of life. Why do we slip backward when we want so much to forge ahead?

Why do we slip backward when we want so much to forge ahead?

Our "backsliding," as an older generation used to call it, may actually stem from our good intentions and moral endeavors. We have high ideals. We do our duty and give life our best shot. This approach to life is highly recommended by philosophers, moralists, idealists, and a host of other well-intentioned people who foist on us the deceit that goodness can be achieved through holy resolution and hard effort.

Well-intentioned people foist on us the deceit that goodness can be achieved through holy resolution and hard effort.

But it doesn't work, as everyone knows who's tried it. We can't sustain the effort, and in due time we will revert to our old nature: to sexual immorality, impurity, debauchery, idolatry, witchcraft, hatred, discord, jealousy, fits of rage, selfish ambition, dissensions, factions, envy, drunkenness, orgies, and all the other manifestations of the flesh (see Galatians 5:21).

No, the flesh can't help us go forward. It can only take us back. Radical as the concept may sound, the only way to deal with our flesh is to kill it. We must say with Paul, "I know that nothing good lives in me, that is, in my sinful nature" (Romans 7:18), and turn our attention to God—to worship Him in the beauty of His holiness and allow Him to change us how and when He will. We cannot be good in and of ourselves. "There is only One who is good," declared Jesus (Matthew 19:17).

❧

The flesh can't help us go forward.
It can only take us back.

Theologian and philosopher Helmut Thielicke, in *The Prayer That Spans the World*, puts it this way:

> Holiness does not depend at all on your own exertions and your own inner progress . . . Everything depends on your being willing to honor God and let Him work in your life, simply to stand still and let Him be the "holy one" who will have first place in your life, above all men and all things. Then the other [holiness] will come of itself . . . Luther once spoke of this same effect, saying that one does not need to command a stone which is lying in the sun to be warm; it becomes warm quite of itself.

Or it may be that we revert to the Jacob-life because, as the old love song puts it, "the feeling's gone and [we] just can't get it back." Emotion has subsided, and we suppose, in losing it, that we've lost the ground we've gained. We get discouraged with ourselves and give up.

It can't be repeated too often that the deepest experiences in the Christian life are the result of faith, which may or may not be accompanied by emotion, but which remain when the glow of emotion has faded. "Our own feelings . . . are very poor guides when it comes to the robust realities of the Spirit," says Evelyn Underhill. Feelings come and go, but mostly they go—and this in itself is a God-given grace that trains us to walk by faith and not by sight. When the feeling is gone, the reality remains. We are as we were when we first believed.

The deepest experiences in the Christian
life are the result of faith.

And finally, failure may come because, no matter what we've been taught, our sinful nature still exists. Yet despite our continued lapses into sin, our faith and our utter dependence on God will continue to grow as we learn through daily experience that He is completely trustworthy. As we mature in Christ we also get to know ourselves better (including the depths to which our depravity can drag us), and thus we become inclined to cling to God more tenaciously and consistently. We don't outgrow our propensity to sin; we can only grow in our ability to hang on to God.

༄

Feelings come and go, but mostly they go.
When the feeling is gone, the reality remains.

God, who has put up with a failed human race for as long as it's been around, deals patiently and lovingly with our reversals and retreats. He loathes our sin but has paid for it at great price. So when we place our trust completely in Jesus Christ and accept His full payment for our sin, our sordid spiritual condition becomes, in effect, a non-issue.

The poet John Donne, preoccupied with his own spiritual regressions, writes:

Wilt Thou forgive that sin where I begun,
Which was my sin, though it were done before?
Wilt Thou forgive that sin through which I run,
    And do run still, though still I do deplore?
When Thou has done, Thou hast not done,
    For I have more.

But then he recalls what Jesus has done on the cross. "And having done that," Donne affirms, "Thou hast done. I fear no more."

Our repeated and habitual relapses are not to be feared. When seen in the light of God's redemptive love and grace, they serve as opportunities for us to see ourselves for who we are and for God to lift us to a place of greater blessing. The debacle at Shechem became the means by which Jacob was drawn to Bethel and to greater intimacy with God.

God wastes nothing and uses everything—even our spiritual regression—to make us whole.

God wastes nothing and uses everything—even our spiritual regression—to make us whole.

～

Then God said to Jacob, "Go up to Bethel and settle there, and build an altar there to God, who appeared to you when you were fleeing from your brother Esau."

So Jacob said to his household and to all who were with him, "Get rid of the foreign gods you have with you, and purify yourselves and change your clothes. Then come, let us go up to Bethel, where I will build an altar to God, who answered me in the day of my distress and who has been with me wherever I have gone." . . .

After Jacob returned from Paddan Aram, God appeared to him again and blessed him. God said to him, "Your name is Jacob, but you will no longer be called Jacob; your name will be Israel . . . A nation and a community of nations will come from you . . . The land I gave to Abraham and Isaac I also give to you, and I will give this land to your descendants after you."

GENESIS 35:1–3, 9–12

(Read Genesis 35:1–15)

Back to Bethel

Then with my waking thoughts, bright with
   Thy praise,
Out of my stony griefs, Bethel I'll raise;
So by my woes to be nearer, my God, to Thee!
Nearer, my God, to Thee; nearer to Thee!
                           —SARAH ADAMS

THERE COMES A grief, a woe—and then a sudden urge to get back to Bethel. We act on impulse, or so we think, when in fact the impulse originates in God, whose loneliness and longing far exceeds ours.

I sought the Lord, and afterward I knew
He moved my soul to seek Him, seeking me;
It was not I that found, O Savior true,
No, I was found of Thee.

                           —ANONYMOUS

So it was for Jacob, whose sojourn at Shechem had broken his heart. "*Then* God said to Jacob, 'Arise, go up to Bethel, and live there; and make an altar there to God, who appeared to you when you fled from your brother Esau'" (Genesis 35:1, emphasis added).

*Jacob was in danger of being destroyed
by the very people to whom he was
commissioned to bring God's salvation.*

Jacob's family had sunk to the level of the sordid culture around them. Given the responsibility of lifting the land from its idolatries, Israel now had its own degraded pantheon. Intended to be a fragrant aroma of God's goodness and grace, Jacob's family, as he put it in bitter colloquy, "stunk up" the place (see Genesis 34:30). Indeed, Jacob was in danger of being destroyed by the very people to whom he was commissioned to bring God's salvation.

At first glance it seems that Jacob's fear of and flight from the Canaanites were merely the result of the violence of his sons. But beyond their odious actions was the presence of idolatry in his camp and his own drift away from the living God. What shame and disgrace for the man who had earnestly built altars to Yahweh.

Jacob was one of the honored patriarchs from

whom Messiah would come. For his own sake, as well as for the sake of a fallen world, it was essential that Jacob put away his idols and come back to God.

∽

The tide of culture carries us
away from godly influences.

We, like Jacob, drift away from God gradually and unconsciously. The tide of culture carries us away from godly influences. We lose our desire to sit at Jesus' feet. Our delight to meet Him in the Word fades. We find ourselves lapsing into old idolatries as strange and vile as those that corrupted us before we were reborn. Like Rachel, we hide these idols for a while (Genesis 31:34), but in the end we bring them out and worship them in plain view.

Israel's idolatry was simple and direct: they worshiped the *Tarpi*, the lusty satyrs of Shechem. Our idolatry is often more subtle and difficult to detect— a strange focus on someone or something other than God. Attractions and distractions other than the true God motivate and master us.

Calvin said our hearts are factories in which we endlessly manufacture idols. The evil, he said, is not that we desire things, but that we desire them inordinately. This is the subtle perversion of idolatry.

The evil is not that we desire things,
but that we desire them inordinately.

What are the ambitions and aspirations we venerate? What are the values we value above all? How much time do we spend making money and making a name for ourselves? How much time do we spend with God?

One way to identify your gods is to observe your reaction when you don't get your heart's desire or when that desire is taken away. You'll know because you'll become self-pitying and bitter instead of submitting to God and longing for His likeness.

What are the values we value above all?

Another way to know your idols is to know your own thoughts, for, as Jesus said, "Where your treasure is, there your heart [mind] will be also" (Matthew 6:21). We treasure most what we think about most of the time. Our last thoughts before we sleep, our first thoughts when we awaken, our reveries throughout the day are spent on the things we treasure and trust. These are the gods that draw us away from God's love.

We treasure most what we think about most of the time.

"No one can serve two masters," Jesus assures us. "Either he will hate the one and love the other, or he will be devoted to the one and despise the other" (Matthew 6:24). He does not say we *should not* love two masters. He says we *cannot*. "One master passion in the breast," wrote Byron, "swallows all the rest."

He does not say we should not *love two masters. He says we* cannot.

Is there some grief in you, some woe, a pining for that elusive "something more"? If so, it may be that an idol stands between you and your Lord. There's only one way back—to bring that god into the open, bury it deep, and walk away from it. If you can't do that, tell God you're *willing* to do it. If you can't say that you're willing, tell Him you're willing to be *made* willing. He'll receive you, however you come.

Then, no matter what, come back to Bethel— back to the place of love and adoration, to the place where you first began. Build an altar on the site where you first built one. Give yourself to God once again. Pray as you used to pray; read the Word as you used to read it. Ask God to open your eyes to see wonderful things in His Book and then to hide those things in your heart.

⁓

Nothing eternal has been lost,
for there is no time in eternity.

So what if you've lost a year or more? Nothing eternal has been lost, for there is no time in eternity. Forget what lies behind; press on to that which lies ahead! God can and will bestow on you the old blessing (see Genesis 35:10–12).

Louise Tarkington wrote for us all when she mused, "I wish there were some wonderful place called the Land of Beginning Again, where all our mistakes and all our heartaches and all of our poor selfish grief could be dropped like a shabby old coat at the door and never put on again."

There is such a place: it is Bethel—where God appeared and said to Jacob, "You will no longer be called Jacob; your name will be Israel" (Genesis 35:10). There He appears to us; there He restores our good name and the blessing we seek.

Bethel, however, is not a one-time event. We must meet God there every day.

> Lord, mend or rather remake us: one creation
>   Will not suffice our turn;
> Except thou make us daily, we shall spurn
>   Our own salvation.
>
> —GEORGE HERBERT

∾

Now Deborah, Rebekah's nurse, died and was buried under the oak below Bethel. So it was named Allon Bacuth . . .

Then they moved on from Bethel. While they were still some distance from Ephrath, Rachel began to give birth and had great difficulty. And as she was having great difficulty in childbirth, the midwife said to her "Don't be afraid, for you have another son." As she breathed her last—for she was dying—she named her son Ben-Oni. But his father named him Benjamin.

So Rachel died and was buried on the way to Ephrath (that is, Bethlehem) . . .

Jacob came home to his father Isaac in Mamre, near Kiriath Arba (that is, Hebron), where Abraham and Isaac had stayed. Isaac lived a hundred and eighty years. Then he breathed his last and died and was gathered to his people, old and full of years. And his sons Esau and Jacob buried him.

GENESIS 35:8, 16–19, 27–29

(Read Genesis 35:8–29)

The Mystery of Sorrow

*Life is very mysterious. Indeed, it would
be inexplicable unless we believed that God
was preparing us for scenes and ministries
that lie beyond the veil of sense in the eternal
world, where highly-tempered spirits will
be required for special service.*
—F. B. MEYER

THERE ARE FOUR great sorrows in these verses. First,
Deborah, Jacob's old nanny and loyal family retainer,
"died and was buried under the oak below Bethel."
The tree forever after was known as "the Oak of
Weeping" (Genesis 35:8).

Then Rachel, Jacob's beloved wife, died in childbirth, living only long enough to enshrine her pain in
her child's name: Ben Oni—"son of my sorrow" (Genesis 35:16–20). Thirty years later, as Jacob himself
lay dying in Egypt, the haunting memory of Rachel's
death came back to him with its old force and pathos.
Jacob could never forget Rachel, and the anguish of
his loss was never assuaged (Genesis 48:7).

Then Jacob's aged father, Isaac, breathed his last, forever frustrating Jacob's efforts to set things right with the man he had so cruelly deceived (Genesis 35:28–29).

In the meantime, Jacob's firstborn, Reuben, the "might and the beginning of his strength," had seduced his father's wife Bilhah (Genesis 35:22). By his sin Reuben forfeited the honor of his status as firstborn and demonstrated the bitter effect of his association with the Canaanites at Shechem. Years later, Jacob cried out in his grief, "You [Reuben] will never excel, for you went up onto your father's bed . . . and defiled it" (Genesis 49:4).

⌒∽

These were only the beginning of Jacob's sorrows. The harder tests were further along.

But these were only the beginning of Jacob's sorrows. The harder tests were further along.

Jacob lived to see his beloved son Judah fall into impurity and ruin (Genesis 38:1–30). Then he watched helplessly as dissension and hatred tore his family to shreds. The older brothers sold their brother Joseph into slavery and brought his bloody,

THE MYSTERY OF SORROW

torn coat to their father as contrived evidence that wild animals had killed him. Jacob, convinced of their complicity, kept that greater grief to himself until he let it slip in one unguarded moment: "*You* have deprived me of my children," he cried (Genesis 42:36, emphasis added).

On the heels of that bereavement came the famine in which Jacob was forced to risk first Simeon and then Benjamin, Rachel's dying gift and the beloved child of his old age. Then Jacob was swept out of his familiar home into a foreign land, fraught with changes that disrupted his familiar and cherished routines.

~

Who cannot sympathize with Jacob
as he laments before Pharaoh,
"My years have been . . . difficult"

And finally, there was the grief of old age with its fading glory and inevitable descent to the grave. Who cannot sympathize with Jacob as he laments before Pharaoh, "My years have been . . . difficult" (Genesis 47:9).

Are there piercing sorrows in *your* life—unrelieved heartache over a protracted illness, a crippling disability, a dysfunctional family, an unfaithful spouse or friend? Is there some grief over what *might* have been?

The question is this: How do you regard these intrusions? Have you grown bitter and resentful against them, against the people who forced them on you, against God? Are you frustrated because your plans have been disrupted? Are you full of bitterness and cynicism because you think some blind fury is against you?

There's a better way. It is the way God's humble saints have always gone. It is to know that Love and Wisdom are guiding you all the way. God is working out His purpose in spite of all that is happening to you. He *is* working—quietly, invisibly, inexorably taking the worst of your life and turning it into good.

He is working—quietly, invisibly,
inexorably taking the worst of your life
and turning it into good.

This is the mystery of sorrow: God works *through* grief to accomplish His will. He permits it to transform our experiences into a much greater good. "Everything is against me!" Jacob cried in a moment of despair (Genesis 42:36). No! "In all things God is working for the good of those who love him, who have been called according to his purpose" (Romans 8:28).

⁓

This is the mystery of sorrow: God works through grief to accomplish His will.

And what "good" is God doing? He is shaping us into men and women whose lives are redolent with beauty and grace. He is teaching us to bear pain without complaint, to endure insult without retaliation, to suffer shame without bitterness, to be content with our lot in life. He is showing us how to be more patient with others, more tolerant of their weaknesses and failures—how to be kinder, gentler men and women, easier to get along with, easier to work with, easier to be around.

Furthermore, once the bitterness is removed from our sorrow, we are able to know God as we've never known Him before. Job said of his misery: "My ears had heard of you but now my eyes have *seen* you" (Job 42:5, emphasis added). In the words of an old Ira Stanphill song, God washes our eyes with tears that we may see.

Sorrow is the means to the end of all things—
God himself. It brings us heart to heart with Him.
Paul said he rejoiced in his sufferings because suffering produced perseverance, proven character, and
hope (Romans 5:3). But more than that, he insisted,
it taught him to "rejoice in God [alone]" (Romans
5:11).

*Sorrow is the means to the end of all
things—God himself.*

When we have been robbed of health, friends,
money, and favorable circumstances, God then
becomes the only thing in life for us. We come to love
Him for himself and not for what He has to give. We
cry out with the psalmist, "Whom have I in heaven
but you? And earth has nothing I desire besides you"
(Psalm 73:25). The path of sorrow has taken us to
the place where God, and God alone, is our praise.

"What do you think of your God now?" asked
a cynic of an old saint, who for twenty years had
endured great physical pain. "I think of him more
than ever," was the reply.

*We come to love [God] Him for himself and
not for what He has to give.*

And then, lest we forget, on ahead lies heaven, where God "will wipe every tear from [our] eyes. There will be no more death or mourning or crying or pain" (Revelation 21:4). The path of pain will have led us to the land where pain is unknown. No grief, only joy, and the service for which we've been fully prepared. This is the sweet aftermath of sorrow.

Then shall those powers which work for grief,
    Enter Thy pay,
    And day by day
Labour Thy praise and my relief:
    With care and courage building me,
    Till I reach heav'n, and much more, *Thee*.

—GEORGE HERBERT

Then Joseph brought his father Jacob in and presented him before Pharaoh. After Jacob blessed Pharaoh, Pharaoh asked him, "How old are you?"

And Jacob said to Pharaoh, "The years of my pilgrimage are a hundred and thirty. My years have been few and difficult, and they do not equal the years of the pilgrimage of my fathers." Then Jacob blessed Pharaoh and went out from his presence.

GENESIS 47:7–10

Making Us Great

The Firste Stok, Fader of Gentilesse—
What man that claymeth gentil for to be
Must followe His trace, and alle His wittes dresse
Vertu to sewe, and vyces for to flee.
For unto vertu longeth dignitee,
And noght the revers, sauffly dar I deme,
*   Al were he mytre, croune, or diademe.*
                    —GEOFFREY CHAUCER

CHAUCER'S POEM, THOUGH his Middle English obscures much of its meaning, tells us that Jesus, our first ancestor, is the father of "gentilesse," a word that meant "nobility" in Chaucer's day. As he put it, those who wish to live noble lives must follow Jesus' path and arrange their thoughts to pursue virtue and flee from vice. "For," Chaucer wrote, "dignity belongs to virtue and not the reverse, I may safely say, whether I wear a [bishop's] mitre, a [king's] crown, or an [emperor's] diadem."

The same theme appears in several of Chaucer's *Canterbury Tales*. His Wife of Bath, for example, insists that whoever behaves nobly is a true gentle-man, regardless of birth, saying in effect, "Genteel is as genteel does" ("He is gentil that doth gentil dedis [deeds]"). That gentility, she insists, is inward and comes from Christ, not men.*

This was heady stuff in the fourteenth century when it was assumed that nobility was solely a matter of lineage and social class. But no human being can bequeath nobility, Chaucer argues, nor can it be appropriated by any class or rank. It comes from Jesus, "the First Father in majesty," who makes whomever He pleases His heirs. Virtue is nobility, and unless we love virtue as Jesus does there is no dignity or majesty in us, regardless of our breeding.

Unless we love virtue as Jesus does there is no dignity or majesty in us.

What does any of this have to do with Jacob? Picture, if you will, a decrepit old man, dressed in the rough and ragged garb of the Bedouin. He is uneducated and unaccustomed to the manners and

---

* I am indebted to medievalist Dr. Barbara Kline for her translation of Chaucer's poem and her insights into its meaning.

protocol of the court. And he is appearing before the most powerful man on earth, the king of Egypt.

One man bears the glory of birth and station, the other the glory of godliness. "One lifts up his head in his own glory; the other says to his God, 'You are my glory and the lifter up of my head.' One delights in his own majesty; the other says to his God, 'I will love Thee, Oh God, my majesty,'" said Augustine.

∽

One lifts up his head in his own glory; the other says to his God, "You are my glory and the lifter up of my head."

Thus Jacob "blessed Pharaoh," and "without doubt the lesser person is blessed by the greater" (Hebrews 7:7).

Jacob was a failure, a ruined man, a welfare case who was utterly dependent on Egypt's largesse. But he was also a man whom God had worked and shaped into godliness. No longer an ordinary man, he was now "Israel"—one who had power with God and humankind (Genesis 32:28). At last, at the end of his days, Jacob was becoming the man he was meant to be—a prince with God.

In the eyes of ordinary men and women, Jacob's brother, Esau, was the greater man. Through the years Esau had accumulated immense wealth and power. He was the ruler of the land of Edom and could have met the ruler of Egypt on his own terms. Yet Esau, with all his earthly authority, could not have blessed Pharaoh. Only Jacob had that power.

This tells us that the spiritual is greater than the natural. God can endow a simple, humble human being with awesome moral force. Holiness has within itself the power to master all other powers. The holy ones, says David, "are the excellent ones" (Psalm 16:3).

∽

Holiness has within itself the power to master all other powers.

It's interesting that the Greek word for authority, *exousia*, actually means "from [our] being," suggesting that the ability to influence others flows from inside out and is rooted in what we *are*. "Do you wish to be great?" Augustine asks. "Then begin by *being*." Greatness comes from holiness and nothing more.

Evelyn Underhill has written:

We mostly spend [our] lives conjugating three verbs: to Want, to Have, and to Do. Craving, clutching, and fussing on the material, political, social, emotional, intellectual—even on the religious plane, we are kept in perpetual unrest, forgetting that none of these verbs have any ultimate significance, except so far as they are transcended by and included in the fundamental verb to Be; and that Being, not wanting, having, and doing, is the essence of life.

I think of a friend who makes his way through the so-called "halls of power" in Washington D.C., meeting with the most prominent and powerful women and men in the world. He speaks a word or two, prays, then passes on, but he leaves behind the lingering and compelling influence of Christ. He's a quiet, humble man, yet he possesses uncanny presence. He has about him that aura of greatness that surrounds all whose lives reflect the character of Jesus. It is the greatness of godliness.

God has one purpose: to make us great. It is a force that transcends earthly power, an authority that has nothing to do with natural birth, lineage, or human pedigree. It is God's legacy to His children, if we will have it.

"Not often does the sap of virtue rise in the branches," Dante said. "This is [God's] gift and we can only ask that he bequeath it."

Then Joseph brought his father Jacob in and presented him before Pharaoh. After Jacob blessed Pharaoh, Pharaoh asked him, "How old are you?"

And Jacob said to Pharaoh, "The years of my pilgrimage are a hundred and thirty. My years have been few and difficult, and they do not equal the years of the pilgrimage of my fathers." Then Jacob blessed Pharaoh and went out from his presence.

So Joseph settled his father and his brothers in Egypt and gave them property in the best part of the land, the district of Rameses, as Pharaoh directed. Joseph also provided his father and his brothers and all his father's household with food, according to the number of their children.

GENESIS 47:7–12

Time Flies

The life of man is hasty.
—Thomas Hobbes

Pharaoh asked Jacob, "How old are you?" Jacob answered, "The years of my pilgrimage are a hundred and thirty. My years have been *few* . . ." (Genesis 47:8–9, italics added). I'm struck by Jacob's length of days and his assessment of their brevity.

"The dash between the dates," that short dash separating the birth and death dates on tombstones, represents the brief span of one's life.

Life's brief span has inspired numerous metaphors in literature: it is a dream, a flying shuttle, a mist, a puff of smoke, a shadow, a gesture in the air, a sentence written in the sand, a bird flying in one window of a house and out another. Perhaps the most apt symbol has been suggested by Joseph Fuiten, who reckons that "the dash between the dates," that short dash separating the birth and death dates on tomb-stones, represents the brief span of one's life.

As we get closer to the end of our days, it moves with increasing swiftness.

When we were children, time loitered. But as we get closer to the end of our days, it moves with increasing swiftness, like water swirling down a drain. In childhood we measured our age in small increments. "I'm six-and-a half," we would say, for it took so long to get older. Now we have no time for such childishness. Who claims to be sixty-and-a-half?

It's good to ponder the brevity of life now and then. I think of Moses' poem and prayer: "Teach us to number our days aright, that we may gain a heart of wisdom" (Psalm 90:12). Life is too short to treat it carelessly.

Life is too short to treat it carelessly.

The country parson George Herbert said he used to frequent graveyards to "take acquaintance of this heap of dust." He wrote:

Dear flesh, while I do pray, learn here thy stem
And true descent; that when thou shalt grow fat
And wanton in thy cravings thou mayest know
That flesh is but the glass which holds the dust
That measures all our time; which also shall
Be crumbled into dust. Mark here below
How tame these ashes are, how free from lust,
That thou mayest fit thyself against the fall.

Herbert found himself in a graveyard and pondered his own death. He pictured "the dust that measures all our time" running through the hourglass of his flesh, which would itself in time become dust and be laid to rest with the ashes of those who lay beneath his feet. "Mark here below [in the grave]," he writes, "how tame these ashes are, how free from lust"—how unmoved by a passion for money, sex, or power.

*Though time is running out, it is never too
late to give ourselves to God.*

It's high time we too take acquaintance of *our* dust, its transient lust, and what alone will last. Peter says we've "spent enough time doing what pagans choose to do"—living for the lusts of the flesh. There's no time now to waste. We must lose ourselves in the will of God (see 1 Peter 4:1–3). Though time is running out, it is never too late to give ourselves to God.

"Old men will dream dreams," Joel said (Joel 2:28), a notion T. S. Eliot echoes in one of his poems:

> Redeem the vision in the high dream.
> Redeem the time; redeem the dream.

Redeem the vision in the high dream. The "low dream" is to live for oneself—the only dream ordinary men and women can understand. The "high dream" is to live for the will of God, the only way to buy up what's left of our days.

Finish the course with beauty, strength, and dignity.

There are those pathetic, impotent old men and women who love only themselves and live solely for this world, who eke out their bitter existence, grimly enduring the futility of their final days. But there are also those elderly folks who determine to live the rest of the time in the flesh no longer for the lusts of men but for the will of God. They finish the course with beauty, strength, and dignity. Though outwardly perishing, their inward person is renewed day by day.

George MacDonald, in *The Seaboard Parish*, writes of this in his typically heartwarming way:

> Dr. [Izaak] Walton said, "There is the same kind of beauty in a good old face that there is in an old church." You can't say the church is so trim and neat as it was in the day that the first blast of the organ filled it with a living soul. The carving is not quite so sharp, the timbers are not quite so clean. There is a good deal of mould and worm-eating and cobwebs about the old place. Yet both you and I think it more beautiful now than it was then. Well, I believe it is, as nearly as possible, the same with an old face. It has got stained, and weather-beaten, and worn; but if the organ of truth has been playing on inside the temple of the Lord, which St. Paul says our bodies are, there is in the old face, though both form and complexion are gone, just the beauty of the music inside. The wrinkles and the brownness can't spoil it. A light shines through it all—that of the indwelling spirit. I wish we all grew old like old churches."

So do I.

Now the Israelites settled in Egypt in the region of Goshen. They acquired property there and were fruitful and increased greatly in number.

Jacob lived in Egypt seventeen years, and the years of his life were a hundred and forty-seven. When the time drew near for Israel to die, he called for his son Joseph and said to him, "If I have found favor in your eyes, put your hand under my thigh and promise that you will show me kindness and faithfulness. Do not bury me in Egypt, but when I rest with my fathers, carry me out of Egypt and bury me where they are buried."

"I will do as you say," he said

"Swear to me," he said. Then Joseph swore to him, and Israel worshiped as he leaned on the top of his staff.

GENESIS 47:27–31

Home at Last!

These seas are tears and heav'n the haven.
—INSCRIPTION ON AN ANCIENT GLOBE

"SOME OF US get rich," says Robert Capon; "some of us get sick; some of us get funny in the head; some of us write books; some of us behave ourselves; some of us live in Grand Rapids. But every last one of us dies." Sooner or later we all descend to decay. Flesh turns to dust, leaving nothing but dry bones.

*Thoughts of death, and indeed death itself,
shadow us throughout our years.*

Thoughts of death, and indeed death itself, shadow us throughout our years. The apostle Paul refers to death as the last enemy to be overcome (1 Corinthians 15:26). Some people are terrified of death and can't surrender to it, but not Jacob. He knew the promise of God—that Abraham's seed would inherit Canaan—and calmly asked to be carried back there and buried with his fathers.

But Jacob also had that faraway look you often see in the eyes of godly old folks when they talk about dying. He saw beyond Canaan to "the city with foundations, whose architect and builder is God," and he "welcomed it from a distance." Jacob, like all good pilgrims, looked for "a better country—a heavenly one" (see Hebrews 11:9–16).

Jacob, like all good pilgrims, looked for "a better country—a heavenly one.

Many people who read the Old Testament never think to look for heaven there, but the logic of God's covenant requires it. Before Israel became a nation, God promised to join himself to the seed of Abraham. "I will take you as my own people and I will be your God," He would tell Jacob's descendants (Exodus 6:7). And as C. S. Lewis observed, "Once a man is joined to God, how can he not live forever?" To this day God *is*—not *was*—the God of Jacob, as Jesus argued so cogently (Matthew 22:31–32). Jacob lives! God is the God of the living, not of the dead.

c✧ɔ

"Once a man is joined to God, how can he
not live forever?" —C. S. Lewis

Heaven makes its presence known throughout
the Old Testament—in symbol and song, in metaphor and type. One of the most convincing pictures
is that of God himself "taking us in."

The idea first occurs in the story of Enoch, who
walked with God for three hundred years and then "was
no more, because *God took him*" (Genesis 5:24, italics added). Enoch and God took a walk one afternoon
and got far from Enoch's house. The old fellow was too
weary to walk all the way home so God took him in.

One of Israel's poets saw himself and others as
"destined for the grave," but comforted himself in
the knowledge that "God . . . will surely *take me* to
himself" (Psalm 49:15, italics added).

Another poet learned God's presence from his
peril. "I am always with you," Asaph concluded. "You
hold me by my right hand; you guide me with your
counsel and afterward you will *take* me into glory"
(Psalm 73:23–26, italics added).

"Taken in." I like that way of looking at my own
death. It reminds me of something Jesus said: "I am

going to prepare a place for you. And if I go and prepare a place for you, I will come back and *take* you to be with me that you also may be where I am" (John 14:2–3, italics added).

This is the fundamental revelation of heaven: being welcomed, acknowledged, received, embraced, and included. Someone is waiting for us—waiting to take us in.

This is the fundamental revelation of heaven: being welcomed, acknowledged, received, embraced, and included. Someone is waiting for us—waiting to take us in. Thus death is less an enemy and more a friend, bringing us into more of God's love and into His eternal purpose for us beyond our earthly life. If we believe that "Christ has indeed been raised from the dead, the firstfruits of those who have fallen asleep" (1 Corinthians 15:20), death has truly lost its lethal sting. We have absolutely nothing to fear—and everything to gain.

Death has truly lost its lethal sting. We have absolutely nothing to fear—and everything to gain.

St. Francis of Assisi speaks of "Sister Death, who brings peace and rest to the weary soul." Age and weariness may make us long for death, as Paul himself confessed in 2 Corinthians 5:8; but that is a matter best left to the Lord. For now, we must bide our time with love and patience, waiting to complete our task here on earth. God knows what is left for us to do, and He will sustain us until it is finished. "We are immortal," said Augustine, "until our work on earth is done."

God knows what is left for us to do, and He will sustain us until it is finished.

The main thing, in the meantime, is to maintain a "next-world" perspective, remembering all the while that this present world is not our home. We are, as the old spiritual reminds us, "just a-passin' through."

Some set their hearts on this time-bound world; others wait for a world that is timeless. The former, deprived in the present, may decide there's nothing left to live for; the latter can endure anything for the knowledge of what lies ahead.

⌒◌

Some set their hearts on this time-bound world;
others wait for a world that is timeless.

My friend and mentor Ray Stedman wrote:

The world tells us, if you don't take it now, you're never going to get another chance. Don't succumb to the philosophy that you have to have it all now or you will never have another chance. You can pass by a lot of things now and be content because you know that what God is sending you now is just what you need to get you ready for what He has waiting for you when this life is over.

I have seen that misunderstanding drive people into forsaking their marriages after thirty or forty years and running off with another, usually younger, person, hoping they can still fulfill their dreams because they feel life is slipping away from them. Christians are not to think that way. This life is a school, a training period where we are being prepared for something that is incredibly great, but is yet to come. I don't understand all that is involved in that, but I believe it, and sometimes I can hardly wait until it happens.

The frustrations and disappointments we inevitably experience in this world are expressions of our God-given desire to have it all. But we cannot have it all in this world. True, there are lavish serendipities and happy surprises in this life, but they're always tinged with sadness—a homesickness we can never quite shake off until we go home. We must content ourselves with modest joys now, knowing that we have title to far more when we leave this life. George Herbert wrote:

> Not that he may not have here
>   Taste of Thy cheer,
> But as birds drink and straight lift up their head
> So must he sip and think of better drink
> He may attain to after he is dead.

I'm reminded of C. S. Lewis's Hrossa in *Out of the Silent Planet*, who drank deeply at Balki the Pool and said to Ransom: "That was the best of drinks save one."

"Which one," asked Ransom.

"Death itself in the day I drink it and go to Maleldil [God]."

Here's the lesson: we go around *twice*, and thus we don't have to go for all the gusto this time around.

We can live contentedly in broken and ruined bodies for a while; we can endure poverty and privation for a time; we can face loneliness, heartache, and pain for a season, for on ahead lies heaven and our final healing—what ancient writers called *athanasias pharmakon* (the medicine that renders us immortal)—God's cure for all that ails us here on earth.

Heaven, not Idaho, is my home. I must remind myself of that fact every day. It is my respite from defeat and thwarted hope, my restitution for all I've loved and lost here on earth, my safe haven from this world's sea of tears.

On ahead lies heaven and our final healing—God's cure for all that ails us here on earth.

Like my father Jacob, I look past this present day and its sorrow to "that great gettin up morning" when "the sun of righteousness will rise with healing in its wings" (Malachi 4:2), when "souls shall wear their new array, and all their bones with beauty shall be clad,"* when I shall dwell, as the psalmist exults, "in

---

* George Herbert

the house of the LORD *forever*!" (Psalm 23:6, italics added).

That is the most cherished tenet of my creed.

Then [Jacob] gave [his sons] these instructions: "I am about to be gathered to my people. Bury me with my fathers in the cave in the field of Ephron the Hittite, the cave in the field of Machpelah, near Mamre in Canaan, which Abraham bought as a burial place from Ephron the Hittite, along with the field. There Abraham and his wife Sarah were buried, there Isaac and his wife Rebekah were buried, and there I buried Leah." . . .

When Jacob had finished giving instructions to his sons, he drew his feet up into the bed, breathed his last and was gathered to his people.

GENESIS 49:29–33

The Cleansing Flame

Purge me, Lord, and give me grace to
bear the heat
of cleansing flame;
not bitter at my lowly lot, but mete
to bear my share of suffering and keep
sweet,
in Jesus' Name.
                    —RUTH BELL GRAHAM

AND SO WE come to the end of Jacob's story. "My years
have been few and difficult," he had once sighed. So it
was for the old patriarch, and so it is for us. Life buf-
fets and restricts us, makes demands on us that we do
not want to bear. Yet we can rejoice in what the years
bring, for God is at work in every aspect of our life,
including our suffering, to create a new person.

Suffering—even the most unjust, undeserved,
and pointless suffering—is an opportunity for us to
respond in such a way that our Lord can, in His good
time, turn us into His own likeness. As James puts it,
we can take heart—no, take *joy* in our trials, because

we know that adversity has worked to make us "mature and complete, not lacking anything" (James 1:3–4).

❧

We long for maturity, but we want the quick fix.

We long for maturity, but we want the quick fix. "Give us Seven Laws," we say, "Eight Habits, Nine Steps for Building a Better Me." But there are no short courses or fast-track programs that can accomplish God's ultimate purpose for us. The only way to grow into Christ's likeness is to submit each day to the conditions that God brings into our lives. It is a matter of laying down our wills and accepting *His* will as it comes to us in the form of the people with whom we live and work, and in the circumstances presented to us each day. We must be willing to do the will of the One we love and follow Him no matter what it costs.

❧

No short courses or fast-track programs can accomplish God's ultimate purpose for us.

Pressure, perplexity, persecution, outward and inward blows may be our frequent lot. We can trivialize our pain and withdraw from it; we can grow bitter, resentful of others, and angry with God; or we can say, "Not my will but yours be done."

~

We must be willing to do the will of the One we love and follow Him no matter what it costs.

That means consenting to displacement, misunderstanding, embarrassment, and loss of esteem. It means embracing debilitating physical or emotional disease, a difficult relationship, even the struggle to overcome a habit of sin until God elects to rid us of its control.

This is our part—an attitude of acceptance that makes it possible for the God who walks beside us to shape and make us into what He has envisioned for us. The process is mysterious and inexplicable, but it is God's way of removing our disfigurements and endowing us with His grace and beauty. As we accept His will and submit to His ways, His holiness becomes ours. Gradually, inexorably, adversity turns us into kinder, gentler folks—sturdier, stronger, more secure and sensible. The beginning is small, but progress is inevitable: "The dawning light grows to noonday."

*As we accept His will and submit to His
ways, His holiness becomes ours.*

This is the end of Jacob's story and of all those who are in his spiritual line. May God give us grace "to bear the heat of cleansing flame, not bitter at our lot, but mete to bear our share of suffering and keep sweet, in Jesus' name."*

Amen.

---

* Emmet Fox, "Your Heart's Desire."

Note to the Reader

THE PUBLISHER INVITES you to share your response to the message of this book by writing Discovery House Publishers, Box 3566, Grand Rapids, MI 49501, USA. For information about other Discovery House books, music, DVDs, or videos, contact us at the same address or call 1-800-653-8333. Find us on the Internet at www.dhp.org or send e-mail to books@dhp.org